ISBN 0-7683-2060-7

Library of Congress Catalog Card Number 98-43022

Text by Flavia and Lisa Weedn
Illustrations by Flavia Weedn
© Weedn Family Trust
www.flavia.com
All rights reserved

Published in 1999 by Cedco Publishing Company
100 Pelican Way, San Rafael, California 94901
For a free catalog of other Cedco® products, please write
to the address above, or visit our website: www.cedco.com

Printed in China

The artwork for each picture is digitally mastered using acrylic on canvas.

With love and gratitude to those kindred spirits whose
dedication, endless support, and talented hands made this book
a reality — Lisa Mansfield, Jane Durand, Diana Musacchio, Tyler
Tomblin, Jennie Sparrow, Solveig Chandler, Kim Gendreau,
Annette Berlin, Hui-Ying Ting-Bornfreund.

To believe is to know

that every day is a new beginning.

It is to trust that miracles happen.

To believe is to find the strength and

courage that live within us when it is

time to pick up the pieces and begin again.

To believe is to know we are never alone,

that life is a gift, and this is our

time to cherish it.

INSIGHTS TO HEALING

To Take
Away the Hurt

Flavia and Lisa Weedn

Illustrated by Flavia Weedn

Cedco Publishing Company • San Rafael, California

Authors' Note

This book is the blending of two generations, that of mother and daughter. Side by side, we offer a deeply personal view into the window of our lives, for each story written is a true account of hope and challenge, faith and vision. Our words are simple, uncluttered, and speak solely from the heart. Our greatest wish is that within the authenticity of our storytelling, you will find a resonating corner, a common thread of understanding, and a reason to believe.

TABLE OF CONTENTS

We have all known hurt. Heartache, like love, is an emotion that proves we exist. Hurt can be a slow, dull ache, or a sharp and not-so-silent void. It can create a stillness in our lives so profound that we can not move – until we come to realize that life is far too precious to remain motionless. Life holds hidden gifts in its hands, and even the most painful of all our experiences can lead us to awakenings that lift us higher and bring us closer to our faith. As we work through our grief, be it loss, change, or disappointment, it is important to know that we are never alone with our feelings and that we are all connected in some

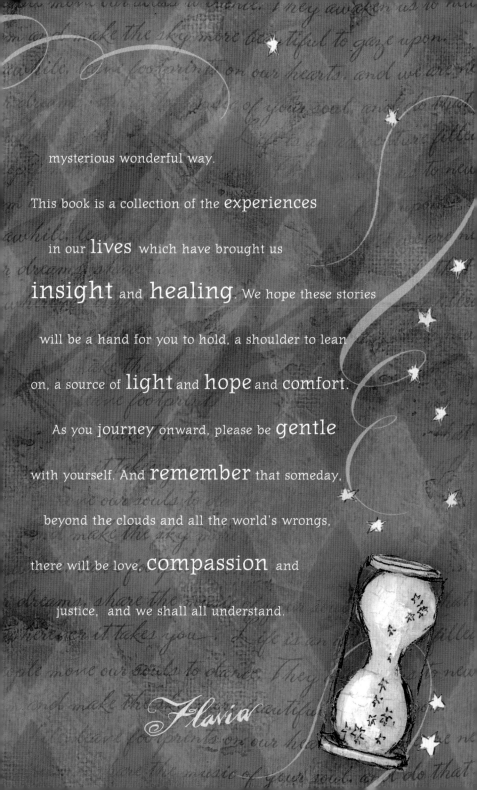

mysterious wonderful way.

This book is a collection of the experiences

in our lives which have brought us

insight and healing. We hope these stories

will be a hand for you to hold, a shoulder to lean

on, a source of light and hope and comfort.

As you journey onward, please be gentle

with yourself. And remember that someday,

beyond the clouds and all the world's wrongs,

there will be love, compassion and

justice, and we shall all understand.

Flavia

I wish I could

take away the hurt

and soothe the

empty places inside

your heart where

tears are born.

The Empty Places

Our lives are

woven by the

weavers of time,

in a pattern we

cannot see.

Patterns

by Flavia Weedn

I believe our lives are tapestries woven from our experiences, including those of great joy and great sorrow. The strongest threads, which hold our tapestries together, are woven from those we love, and from those who have made an impact upon our lives. With time, images and patterns appear, and we begin to see them more clearly.

Mama and I were lost in the sound of silence as we made another trip down the same streets we had driven regularly since her illness had been diagnosed. I hurt so much for her, if I'd voiced that which was in my heart, my words would have been a scream. Just a little further now, I thought. Once we get over this next hill, we'll be at the oncologist's office.

By this time, the thought of getting over one hill at a time was indelible in my mind. It was the day-to-day pattern we had chosen from the beginning — the only way my brother, sister and I knew how to support each other and walk with Mama until she was rid of this terrible disease. It was the bridge of hope we had built to connect each of the new medications and

13

treatments the doctors deemed necessary. In all probability, it was the only reason that kept us from lashing out at the world. As we tried desperately to give our combined strengths to her, Mama valiantly climbed every hill put before her.

She was a strong and vital woman, who loved life so much she tasted it. Her courage and faith were indescribable. She, as well as the rest of us, always believed she would win her battle with this dreadful illness. While she was in and out of the hospital, we consulted with doctors, societies and foundations in a quest to learn and understand more about this war she was fighting. But our faith, presence, love and prayers seemed all my brother, sister and I had to give, and we struggled with the helplessness we felt.

A short month later, while at home, she asked me to sit on the bed beside her, said we needed to talk. She told me how she wanted her personal belongings to be divided between the three of us. And as she went through her list, the finality of the moment began to break my heart.

I didn't understand. How could it be that outside her window, the sun was still in the sky, her flowers still bloomed, and people walking by were still laughing and talking? How could everything just keep going on as usual? Didn't it make any difference? Didn't they know that she was here in this room saying goodbye

to me, to her life, and to this world she loved so much?

I didn't want to hear her reading from some list, how she wanted to give away things which I knew were a part of her. I didn't want any of it. Not the ring she wore as a girl — not her earrings — not the chair Mrs. Whitney had given her — and not the antique dresser we'd found in the thrift store. I couldn't believe this was really happening. I couldn't accept the words she was saying. The only thing I wanted and prayed for was for her to get better, so we could end this nightmare. I wanted Mama back the way she was.

When I calmed down and saw how necessary this conversation was to her, I realized if she were able to talk about it, certainly I could find the strength to hold back my tears. So I listened. And I wrote it all down.

Mama said it was important for us to put away our unanswered questions and anger, for life was a pattern that always unfolded the way it was meant to. She told me there were no more hills for her to climb, and she wanted us to end the heartache. For the time remaining she wanted us to join her in celebrating life and all we'd shared together. During those moments, I listened with my heart, and my love and pride for her became greater than the pain I felt.

Several weeks after Mama died, my brother, sister and I followed her wishes and divided things as she had wanted. In addition, we kept small things each of us had closely associated with her. For me, it was the scissors from her sewing basket, something I had seen her use so often. As I was putting the scissors away, I glanced at the inscription etched into the steel on one side. It read: *The Very Best.* I heard myself answer, "Yes, she was."

Among fabrics folded away in a drawer, I discovered some old patterns she'd made from newspapers. They made me remember that Mama believed anything was possible, and if it were in our power, we should find a way to make it happen. For sewing on cloth, she used her paper patterns to find her way. For anything else, she taught us to use our hearts.

And so we did. We used our hearts to find our separate ways through the emptiness we felt without her. Through time, my brother found her presence in listening to the music she loved. My sister felt Mama's closeness in her kitchen when she cooked with her recipes. I felt her with me in my work with colors, designs and the love of creating we both shared.

One afternoon I told both my sister and my brother how strongly I had felt Mama's presence the day before. In unison they replied that she couldn't have been with me, because she was with them. I realized then that Mama had found some wonderful way to be with each of us while we tried to mend our hearts.

We couldn't see her the way we used to, but I knew

she hadn't really left us, for she was with each of us whenever we thought of her. Mama, herself, was our support during the difficult time following her death. And she is still, even to this day, through the strong bond of love and faith, and the set of beliefs she'd given us. More and more I have realized her strength through the years, and know the beliefs she shared with me were life's truths.

I continue to weave my tapestry, and now its patterns go far back in time, for much has happened since it was begun. The small, golden, unfinished designs touch those that are deep and beautiful, woven from great adventures and quiet victories. Colors that make up a pattern of healing pull away the curtains of darkness and show sorrow as a part of living and death as a part of life.

Threads of joys, dreams, and gratitude make up the radiant colored patterns, while strands of miracles intermingle among those of dreams, memories and change. But the pattern that shines the brightest and the strongest is the one woven from those I love and from those who love me. I believe we find a way to weave together forever that which really matters in our lives.

Be not blue, for

if you look you

shall find me.

I will be translucent,

flickering wings

between the sun

and sky.

Flight of the Sparrow

by Lisa Weedn

I wake to a velvet sky. Gray and smooth its blanket, the air cool and damp. I can taste the salty breeze of the ocean. For a moment I forget.

I look out the window and breathe in the beauty. Then all at once I remember. My heart floods with a heavy weight. I force my body out of bed and splash water on my face, thinking maybe I can wash away the hurt, the unfairness of it all. But I am unsuccessful.

I inch my way to the kitchen. Put the teakettle on. I am so acutely aware of the silence. I can think of nothing but him, and the way his beautiful face belies his weakened body. His eyes still shimmering, in spite of the medication and the pain. His smile still radiating hope, never letting others see the impending question. I reflect upon his hands and the softness I felt only last night when I gave him the treasure I had found. It was a compass with angel wings welded to its sides. I thought it a tender way of saying "Fear not, you're being protected on your path," yet his knowing glance revealed even more, for his eyes told me that soon it would be time to say goodbye. I remember looking back at him, my heart silently screaming, "Not yet, not yet."

The teakettle whistles and I'm shaken from last night's memory. I spy a pale blue bottle resting on the window sill. The soft morning sun finds its way through the clouds, piercing only this particular glass upon the shelf. The bottle, old and delicate, found in a thrift shop long ago, is beckoning me. I'm captured by its simple beauty and the reflection it brings. I tell myself I'll give him this bottle today because it matches the clarity of his eyes. I'll fill it with a freshly picked flower, his favorite. Then I remember I've never asked him what his favorite flower is. There is so much I've never asked. There's not been enough time. God, please let there be more time.

My thoughts are interrupted by the ring of the telephone. I glance over at the clock. It claims an hour too early for a call anything less than urgent. Somehow in my heart I know. "He's gone," is all the shattered voice on the other end of the line says. A wall of tears is my immediate response, followed by that awkward empty space that comes when feelings are too big, too loud for words. We share a silent prayer and then finally whisper our offerings of love. In sync we proclaim, "He's at peace now." But as much as we believe this to be true, it doesn't take away the sharpness of the ache, the shadow of the sadness, or the loss of light all of us who love him are feeling at this moment.

I hang up the phone and feel the conscious ripping of my heart. I want to reach out and hold all the people I love and never let them go. I want to be held by someone wiser than me and be told everything is all right. But mostly I want to reach out to him. I need to tell him what he means to me and how deeply he's touched my life. I just want a moment back to say all the things I never had time to say. I feel the entanglement of grief and anger. I find myself feeling the loss of all the years I didn't know him, and the unfairness of the thief who stole the future.

I hear the ticking of the clock amid the deafening silence, underlining life's fleeting moment. I stand and wipe the tears from my eyes. I grow angry at myself for selfishly feeling this much. I was only his friend. I think about the love of his life, his father, his sister. I should be holding them right now. Trembling, I begin to contemplate God, my faith, my thoughts of heaven. I smell the raspberry scent of my tea and breathe in deeply. I'm overcome with the vision of his eyes, and I remember vividly his last words to me. "I'll watch over all of you when the time comes. You'll feel me. You'll know. Don't forget."

Tears come again and I fold my hands in prayer. I begin to say out loud everything my heart longs to say.

The well overflows, and I speak of the memories and the gifts he brought to my soul. I speak of the things I wish I'd been able to say and do, and how dearly I honor the blessing of his friendship. I vow to watch over his beloved in whatever way I can, and I promise to fill that pale blue glass with the most beautiful flower I can find. I think of the angel compass and I pray he's found his way.

And then I hear a flutter. I think I'm dreaming or imagining it, so I continue with my prayer until I feel a rush of air pass by me. I look up to see a tiny sparrow fly across the room, taking refuge on the window sill, next to the blue glass. Its eyes reflect the newness of the morning sun. I smile in awe and cautiously stand. It appears unafraid and stares back at me. I walk closer, so sure that it will be startled and flee. But it stays calm. Steadfast. As if it has a reason, a definite purpose for being here.

I'm less than a foot away now and I can see its soft feathers and the steady beat of its heart. I'm as locked in its gaze as it appears to be in mine. I extend my hand, sensing a miracle in this moment, and I am not disappointed. The tiny sparrow flies onto my hand. Tiny feet cradle my finger. It is a natural feeling, filled with peace.

I realize this delicate sparrow is a creature of God, a spirit of love meant to soar the heavens, no different from my friend. And this morning, under a velvet sky, it is a messenger sent to remind me.

I slowly walk through the open door and out to the garden. I lift my hand, and believe I see the sparrow hesitate just before it begins its upward flight. My tears turn to grace and gratitude as I whisper skyward, "You're free now. Fly with the angels."

I am at once reawakened.

I can taste the salty breeze of the ocean again, as I breathe in the beauty of love and the miracle of life. I remember that it's not the amount of time we are given, but the richness of the moments shared. For this, I know I have been blessed. I pick the most radiant flower in the garden, and I make the promise to never, ever forget.

Some people

come into our lives

and quickly go.

Some stay for awhile,

leave footprints on

our hearts, and we

are never, ever

the same.

A Song for Him

by Flavia Weedn

It was found taped to the inside of his locker on an Air Force base in England, January of 1945. Just a few words he had jotted down in pencil on a small scrap of paper — part of a poem he had written. Jack, the pilot of a B-17 bomber called the *Lady Be Good*, was twenty-one years old.

The note was small, folded, and had gone unnoticed all these years as it lay hidden among his personal effects sent to us by the War Department over fifty years ago. I unfolded the piece of paper and read Jack's words. "I don't want to leave just yet . . . there are too many books to write . . . too many songs to sing . . . a thousand moons in the sky . . . a million stars to see."

Everything that showed Jack had given up his life for his country, his family, and what he believed in now lies high on a shelf in my studio, inside a blue-green suitcase with a broken handle. But there are unspoken words waiting to be heard, too important to fit in that suitcase. Words of undying strength, integrity and honor. Within the futility of war, there is a story that needs to be told about the courage of the human spirit.

Jack, this song is for you.

৵

On Sunday, December 7, 1941 the news on the radio told us that a place called Pearl Harbor had been bombed. With that announcement, America was at war, and we knew nothing in our world would ever be the same. Soon a new kind of patriotism was born in this country. Single, young men everywhere were enlisting, Jack among them. He enlisted in the Army Air Corps.

He was my mother's younger brother, six years older than I. But to me, he was my big brother, my mentor, my best friend. One night shortly before he left for training, Jack and I sat on the porch steps and talked about life, love, and the strength found in believing. At his young age, he had an insight into the incredibility of life and embraced the hope and courage of the human spirit within the common man. He was my hero, and that night, without realizing it, he gave my heart a reason to believe.

Jack had always dreamed of flying. In describing his first moments in the air, he said he felt so close to heaven that he remembered thinking how amazingly beautiful the world must look to God. Being in the air had been a spiritual experience for him.

26

But those experiences were cut short, for the war was escalating. Everything and everyone was being pushed through the service at a rapid pace. He completed his training, became a pilot, and was sent to England to fly B-17 Flying Fortresses.

At home, we did what other families were doing all across the country. We said goodbye to someone we loved and cherished — too scared to even think we might really be saying goodbye. In Jack's honor, we hung a white satin banner with a blue star in the window. We wrote to him, prayed for his safety, loved him and wanted him back. I missed him with my heart and soul, and at night told God I secretly wondered what I would ever do without him.

In December 1944 the war in the air was at a fierce pitch in Europe. Jack's letters became few, and when he found time to write, he said only that he loved us, thought about us more than ever, and that he'd be home before his birthday in March.

In the early morning hours of that New Year's Eve, Jack took off from his base, Deopham Green, to face a heavy air battle in the sky. It was his thirty-fourth mission — his next to last before coming home. His original crew was with him, except for three new gunners. One of the greatest fears for a new gunner was being trapped inside the plane, unable to get out if the pilot gave the orders to bail; aware of this, Jack promised he would never leave the plane without them.

Two weeks later he was reported missing in action. His was one of five B-17s that had never returned to the base after that mission. Devastated, we prayed for a mistake or some horrible mix-up. We cried out for information, yet were hesitant to read the reports as they were given to us, for fear one would be the one we dreaded most. When we learned that after his plane was hit, four parachutes were seen to have opened, we clung to the hope that one parachute was Jack's.

In the dark weeks that followed, we were in contact with the families of his crew. It made no difference whether the letters were written on monogrammed stationery or on writing tablets purchased in grocery stores, the content was the same. The families all told simple, but heartfelt stories of times remembered. Woven within each was the shining love they had for their sons, and the same heartache that we felt.

Though strangers, we all developed a kindred closeness of heart and spirit during the next two months. Hope somehow bound us together, and we found the strength to await news as to which four of the nine crew members were alive.

In late March, we were notified Jack was killed during that New Year's Eve flight over Germany. With his plane heavily damaged by fifteen to twenty enemy fighters, and burning out of control, Jack dropped out of formation. Knowing there were only seconds remaining before the plane exploded, he gave his crew the order to bail. His co-pilot, navigator, bombardier, and radio operator parachuted to safety. With the autopilot and radio both out, Jack was unable to reach the gunners to see if they were alive. The last crew member to leave the plane told us that just before he bailed out, he looked back to see if Jack was behind him. Instead he saw Jack still at the controls, trying to hold the plane steady so they could jump. Moments later the plane exploded.

Later we learned from the surviving crew that months earlier Jack had been forced to crash-land his huge, damaged B-17 in a small field in Russia. Seeing the size of the area, the crew had shouted, "You'll never make it . . . what makes you think you can?" Jack, holding tightly to the controls, answered, "Because I have to."

꒦

When I think of Jack's story in the tragedy of World War II, my memories fade to black and white and I see it like a film — one in which I cry deeply at the end, with tears of love, humility and pride. To the war, Jack became a statistic, one among many of those unsung ordinary heroes. He may have fought and died in that war, but he didn't belong to it. Jack was more than that. He had a life and a family and dreams, a hometown, and a girl who loved and waited for him.

To me, he's still that young man on the porch steps that night who taught me to see the wonder in life, to love with all my heart, and to be unafraid to stand for what I believe in. He became my own hero years ago, the one who changed my life and taught me to dream, the one who lives in my heart and forever will.

Sadness and emptiness

are difficult to bear,

but that which brings

us sadness

has once brought us joy.

Cherish all that

was yours.

Soulful Awakenings

The words we

most want to say

are difficult to find

sometimes,

for their journey

begins far, far away

in the heart.

Message in a Bottle

by Flavia Weedn

I sit alone in a laundromat. I thought I'd put away the hurt and shed my last tear, yet here I am still thinking about my dad. For eighty years, Daddy had led a colorful and interesting life, doing exactly what he wanted to do. He couldn't have asked for more. I keep telling myself I need to let go of the sadness I feel and think about something else.

Why didn't I just pack Daddy's clothes into a box when we closed his apartment — why am I in this place washing his clothes? Every turning and tossing motion of the dryer only reminds me more of the way he lived his life. Suddenly, it occurs to me that maybe Daddy's the reason I'm in this laundromat. Maybe I've come here to finally say goodbye.

My dad never stayed anywhere for very long, especially home. He was in and out of my life from the time I was eight. Called himself a construction stiff, said he had to be on the move, had the world to see. During most of those years, he took eighteen-month construction jobs overseas, and he saw the world.

He was an alcoholic, and most of my growing-up years were wrapped in wishing for the sober times. When he came home in between jobs, I felt he was making an appearance in our lives — he felt he was on holiday, and he drank. I was embarrassed, ashamed, and lived in fear that one of my friends would see or hear him, so I made excuses why they couldn't come to our house. Looking back, I remember how often during those visits I wished he would leave.

On the surface, when he was sober, and to those who knew him slightly, he was this colorful, humorous, unforgettable character called *Senator*; a mystery writer, adventurer, soldier of fortune, world traveler. His most prized possession was an aluminum suitcase covered with travel and baggage labels. It was very important for him to show people how far and how frequently he'd traveled. My dad had redefined himself long ago. Where he'd been and what he'd done was who he was — and that's what proved he existed. His passport was his business card, and he wore it like a badge.

At airport terminals he needed spectators and lived for that moment. When my dad walked through the gate with other arriving passengers, he was on stage. Among his costumes were turbans, oriental robes, safari helmets, cummerbunds, and sunglasses. Sometimes we had difficulty recognizing him. Other times he was not on the flight at all, having been bumped from the plane in Hawaii for being drunk.

Showman that he was, he gloried when waiting passengers would take photos of him, especially with flashes, for this brought him added attention. He knew they would think they had stumbled upon the arrival of a world-famous dignitary, a celebrity, or an undercover somebody. He would bow and mumble something in a phony accent. He knew in those few moments he had gifted them with a mystery to take home and talk about, and he was the leading character. He loved it.

But what the public saw, and what we, his family, lived with were very different. All through those years, there had been empty places in my childhood I wanted Daddy to fill. I wanted him to give back all the times he wasn't there for me when I needed him and needed him sober. He was my father, and I wanted him to be like other dads. But Daddy had stolen time from me, and now all he had left me to remember him by were scattered moments.

I knew I couldn't change the past, and before tonight, thought I had tied all those unhappy times into bunches and put them away. I must stop my mind from remembering and stop this gnawing ache in my heart. The clothes are dry, and I begin to fold them on the table in front of me. I begin to realize that Daddy had gone in his own direction — he was who he was, nothing more, but nothing less. Unable to give time, all my dad knew how to give were moments.

Tears fill my eyes, and I remember that in many of the moments he gave me, there had been wonder.

☙

It was my nineteenth birthday. I was in class at City College when I was summoned to the administration office. A very large wooden crate addressed to me had been sent from Saudi Arabia. I opened it to an audience and unwrapped a wine-colored leather camel saddle. "Happy Birthday, Babe," the card read, "Love ya, Dad."

☙

My brother, sister and I were young. We watched Daddy carefully fill three balloons with gas from the living room gas jet. He wrote our names and the date on bits of paper and placed one inside each balloon, tied string around the knots in the balloons, and took us outside. He told us on the count of three to let go of the strings. We did, and the balloons flew upward for as far as we could see. Daddy said they would stay there forever and become part of the sky. We stood there motionless, looking up until the balloons disappeared from sight.

☙

We were a little older and riding the Red Car, the trolley that went to the beach. Daddy had a bag on his lap which he kept closed, said it was a surprise. We arrived, walked to the edge of the water, and sat on the sand. He opened the bag and showed us three empty soda pop bottles. He wrote our names and addresses on bits of paper, then added: "Please let me know if you receive this." He placed the notes inside the bottles and told us that bottles could travel like this forever, and the messages could reach places we could never imagine. We watched the three bottles separate as they floated further and further out into the ocean. Daddy said that each would follow its own direction, go its own way, just like people.

꒜

I fold the clothes and put them away, along with all the sadness I brought with me. I leave the laundromat and head for home. For the first time since my dad's death, my heart feels free when I think of him.

If I could, I'd send Daddy a message in a bottle and tell him I filled all the empty places tonight — filled them with the moments of wonder he'd given me. I can almost hear him answer back. *"Thanks, Babe. I love ya. Can't stay long . . . only have a moment."*

Saying a final goodbye to a parent or anyone you love sometimes takes more than words; it takes forgiveness and understanding. I've learned that nothing keeps sadness in our hearts more than words left unsaid. I think of the good times, and now am filled with the realization that it's love and the precious gathered moments that we remember in this life.

The gifts

we receive

are not always

those wrapped

in ribbons,

some are born

of the heart.

Humming the Tune

by Flavia Weedn

There are people in life who allow us to see in vivid colors. Their actions, their personalities, both peculiar and charming, and their unique and wonderful behavior have the power to open up a kaleidoscope of vision. Breaking the monotone view, they bring interest and variety into our lives.

Aunt Mary was such a person — a colorful, naive individual whom her family loved dearly, and at the same time found oddly, affectionately intriguing. She was a petite woman who moved around the room like an inconsistent spark. Flittering. Fluttering. Proud was she. Often she could be caught stealing a glance at her own reflection in the sheen of a chrome toaster or in the clarity of a window pane.

She privately enjoyed the curve of her smile, the bat of her eyes, the sweep of her well-coiffed hair. She'd explore various movements of her hands, which often had the tip of a chiffon scarf or fine handkerchief tucked underneath the grip of a finger ring. The move of her body was carefully poised to fit her changing moods.

One thing was always predictable: she'd deliberately pause, as if pondering on something of great importance, an exquisitely profound memory or thought — just in case another might be watching. Which, of course, is exactly what she hoped for.

Mary just wanted to be noticed. In a delightful and bittersweet way, she was saucy and vain. She was dramatic, could have been a star in films, except she wouldn't have allowed anyone but herself to direct. She belonged in another time and place. Born in Denton, Texas to a large family whose only riches were the deep love they shared, Mary longed to be somebody.

In her twenties, her brief stint as a hairdresser working for Mrs. Snodgrass' beauty parlor was her only claim to fame. But with her chin cocked upward and a mischievous little smirk on her lips, she told people she was born of royalty. Southern royalty, said she, referring to an ancestral Colonel in the Confederate Army during the Civil War. Mary was not elegant, but she did have the grace that comes with a sense of Southern pride, and she proudly believed that Texas would always be the heart of the South.

She had a penchant for profanity and incessantly hummed tunes with no lyrics. Her songs floated from room to room and revealed exactly the kind of mood she was in. Sometimes her pitch was low and thought-provoking, sometimes an anxious tone revealing her unspoken disapproval of the moment, or of an unfairness she had witnessed. We believed she was unaware that her humming was constant, no matter where she was. None of us ever wanted to embarrass or hurt her, so we agreed it was just one of her eccentricities, and we honored her privacy.

Mary liked to travel. The early years brought cruise ships and first-class railroad adventures. In later years, it was Greyhound buses and long car rides. She liked going places just to say she'd been there. Activities were far less important than coming home with the right matchbook, the perfect souvenir plate, the tchotchke spoon dish, or sending home the right postcard. Sometimes she'd send a postcard to herself, just so she had proof. The highest point of each trip was always afterwards, when she could tell us all about it. It was one of the few times Mary didn't hum.

She was big on photo albums, but in an unusual way. Turning the pages, we would discover cutout faces, cutout heads, or even entire cutout people. If she thought anyone looked better than she did, she'd remove their memory with a pair of scissors. Mary would cut out herself only if her family looked good and she thought she didn't. She recorded her life in pictures, most of which revealed small, unevenly cutout faceless people with no explanations or notations as to who the people were.

45

Mary had a great love and intense loyalty for her family. Like many Southern women, the strength of her spirit belied her size, and when needed, she was there to defend or protect any of us in a minute. She was psychic, saw things in dreams before they happened, but only concerning her family or those she loved. She tried to prevent the outcome of these events, but no matter what she'd do, it never changed. This unwanted ability continued on for years, often causing her great heartache.

She worried that if her husband Howard outlived her, his family would get all her treasures. To avoid this, she wrote either my mother's name or mine, in bright red nail polish, on all of the possessions she valued that wouldn't fit in her cedar chest.

As a child, I grew up believing her cedar chest would hold the finest treasures ever imagined. I thought it held the answers to the mysteries of life. I yearned for a peek — just to see one of the things she had wrapped in tissue and ribbon and hidden inside. Whenever I asked, she always answered me by saying that after she was in heaven, then I could open it and touch it all.

"You'll see, it'll be worth the wait," she would say. "It's almost full, and everything in it will be my gift to all of you, after I'm gone. They are the things you will keep to remember me."

Mary died this year at ninety-six. On her insurance papers, she had listed her occupation as "cosmetologist." She had managed to not only outlive Howard by thirty years, but to take her pride with her to heaven. The entire contents of her cedar chest were stolen before she died. We knew it included letters she had written to all of us, her personal and family mementos, diaries of her dreams, her wedding dress, and all of her 1930's costume jewelry. Whatever else there was remained her secret.

I now have the ceramic pitchers, figurines, vases, and powder boxes marked in nail polish, and I am reminded of Mary's distinct style each time I look at her leopard purse, chiffon scarves, and her fancy umbrella.

I hope Mary knows that what I remember most lovingly about her was how she taught me to iron the back of a shirt; how she put too much mayo in her tuna sandwiches; how she would wait for me on the corner when it was dark; and how she'd take me on sightseeing bus tours through Hollywood. I remember her letting me read stories from *True Romance* on Saturday nights and letting me fill the lazy Susan on her chrome table, even though she knew there would be no guests. She'd whisper to me her greatest secrets and confide in me that her heroine was *Gone With the Wind's* Scarlett O'Hara, and that someday she thought the South would rise again.

In the grand plan of things, Aunt Mary was a somebody. She was an unforgettable lady, a real Southern steel magnolia. I loved her dearly, and as I write this I can see her empty cedar chest at the foot of my bed and can almost hear her humming in approval.

❧

$\mathcal{T}$he silent tears

of the heart hurt

the most.

Tell me of your

hurt and my

heart will listen.

Unbroken Dreams

by Flavia Weedn

I grew up believing in dreams. As a child, my dream was to some day have children. I remember looking into the night sky and believing angels were watching over my unborn babies until it was time for them to become a part of my life.

Years later, when I first learned I was going to have a baby, I wanted to stop strangers on the street and tell them. I was absolutely filled with love.

I was in disbelief when months later my baby boy died soon after his birth. I felt the first crack in my dream, and thought my twenty-five-year-old heart would break. The love which had filled my heart so completely had suddenly turned into emptiness, and I was touched with the reality that life is too brief and fragile.

My second little boy was born the next year, also prematurely, and like his brother before him, he lived only a short time. It was a different place, a different time, but the same deep heartache and darkness returned to my world. A part of me had died with each of these babies, and there were no words to explain how I felt. I kept my heart closed, my feelings unshared, and my silent hurt buried deep inside.

I had not yet learned that from every loss there is something gained. Living through the loss of a child can lead us to a deeper knowledge of life's gifts, and a kind of strength we never knew we had. The time came when I could no longer dwell on questions which had no answers, and I searched for insight and a rite of passage to change my focus toward positive memories and feelings. My healing began when I realized I could not have felt this sadness about losing my babies unless I had first been blessed with the joy of loving and wanting them. The real emptiness in my heart would have been never having had them at all.

As I worked through my grief, I was beginning to learn some of life's lessons. The pain of losing someone we love, especially a child, never really leaves us, for it is a part of our lives that will always be unfinished and unexplained. It's never easy to accept the unfairness of life, and yet it touches us all. And sometimes, only because life has touched us in this way, do we become more aware of its wonder and the pure blessing life gives us.

I came to understand that each time I had allowed myself to love, it meant taking a risk. And each time I had reached for a dream also meant taking a risk. I knew the only way I could live life fully was to let go of the emptiness and become unafraid to risk again. I promised myself that I would let love back into my heart, for it is much too precious a gift to waste, and my days and nights too precious to be covered with sadness. I began to cherish life even more.

My third baby son was born the next year, and two years later, my baby daughter. Both again premature, but thanks to God, a wonderfully dedicated pediatrician, and advanced medical technology, they survived. Their hospital stays were long and filled with frightening moments, but in spite of the odds that faced them, they clung tightly to life. Months later when they came home, I slowly found I was mending my broken dreams with the love I was giving to them. And I was beginning a new dream.

Many years have passed, yet the thought of unfairness still comes, and I still feel my tears when I think of my first two babies, or when I hear of precious children being abused and neglected. This is when I remember the lessons I have learned and, instead of dwelling on loss, I strive to embrace the hope I know is real. I now give my love and support to organizations that dedicate themselves to the lives of children and to mending their broken dreams. Giving of myself is the only way I can ever give back the blessings life has given me.

We all have something to give, and it is through this act of giving and risking to love again that we ultimately find a way to heal. Often we uncover sacred gifts of our own just by listening to others who are hurting, or by holding someone's hand and letting them know we care. Each of us has a story, and each of us feels alone with our heartache. Yet we are never truly alone when we let ourselves be unafraid to share our feelings and to give what is in our hearts. Sharing connects us and makes us realize how much people need one another in this world.

I still look up into the night sky sometimes and think about those two little boys that were with me for such a short while. And sometimes I find myself wondering what they would be like today if they could have grown up with their brother and sister. Then I remember that although they are with the angels, in some wonderful way they are still with me — because love never dies. It is the strength we carry with us forever.

The purest wonder in life is found in the sharing of love. And the real gift is to have known love at all. Blessed are we who have held the gift in our hands.

There are

no endings

in life,

only new

beginnings.

Closing Doors, Opening Windows

by Flavia Weedn

*H*e was long out of sight. She stood frozen at the wooden gate, still looking at the curved path in front of her where he'd walked away and at the end of the street where his car had turned and finally disappeared. She paused in hesitation, distancing herself from the moment she dreaded most — going back into the house alone and closing the door.

Forty years of marriage was a lifetime. How could he just drive away from it — and how could she stay in it alone? This was a parting, yet she was the only one who wept, for he was already on his way to somewhere else. If there had been a memory she could have erased, it would have been this one — the day he left and she stayed.

She knew whatever this was, it had begun long ago, and this was the solution he had chosen. Inside she knew it had to end, but this was not the way she'd envisioned it. This closure was too abrupt, too quick, too superficial. A lot of history is lived in forty years, long enough to warrant a few words more than the moment it takes to say goodbye. There were a thousand things she wanted to say that would now remain unsaid. The absence of words. This was the real sadness, this is what she grieved for most.

She walked up the steps and into the house. The sound of the door closing behind her seemed permanent. From habit, she turned and locked it. She took no time to think — had to fill her mind quickly with other things, keep herself busy and occupied until she could let go of the pain and of the empty feeling wrapped around her. While filling her hours with mundane household chores, she lost herself in radio love songs and was able to make it through the first day. When night came, she felt drained and deeply welcomed the tiredness that engulfed her when she fell into bed.

She filled all the new days with busyness and drifted through the time which followed by losing herself in her work. She held on tightly to an invisible rope, for fear if she let go she would break. In the silence of her nights, she thought about her life and where it had brought her thus far. More than half of it had been filled with marriage, raising children, tending to a home, and working at her profession. She had invested herself, her love, her dreams and hopes in all those years. She had worked and loved it all with a passion, and knew she had been loved in return. Family and work, in that order, had been everything to her. Always would be.

And now, change. At first, she had been caught up in the idea that her life would somehow end because everything as she knew it was changing. But she was aware now that this was not so. Although her children were grown, they were loving and supportive, and together they were still a family. It was necessary that her work load increase, but she faced work not as a place to get lost, but rather a place to enjoy. The way she used to.

Time had become her best friend because through it she was learning more about herself. What was really important to her was becoming more defined, more apparent. She had renewed her sense of substance, purpose, and value. Slowly, through the days and nights that followed, her anger diminished, and she began to feel relief.

Whatever degree of failure in her marriage she had felt earlier had faded away and was being replaced by a strength coming from where the emptiness once had been. Freedom had replaced the feeling of unfairness she had harbored. She began to see that change was what she had feared most, and yet when the pieces of change were put together, they became growth.

She may have lost a husband, but through this loss she had found a part of herself she had forgotten existed. Her sense of identity and self-esteem was returning. She had learned through passage that transition is a part of life, that it is not an ending, it is a beginning.

She still believed that the sharing of real love with someone is the closest and greatest gift life can bestow. But change had come, and with it the knowledge that no one can ever depend on another for complete happiness. For that is not life's plan. She knew that each of us finds and makes our own happiness from a place within. She was okay now, and unafraid to begin again.

As she passed by the window, she saw her reflection. A woman who, keeping the best of yesterday, looked forward to each moment of her tomorrows. She opened the window to see where she was going and to let in the rest of her life.

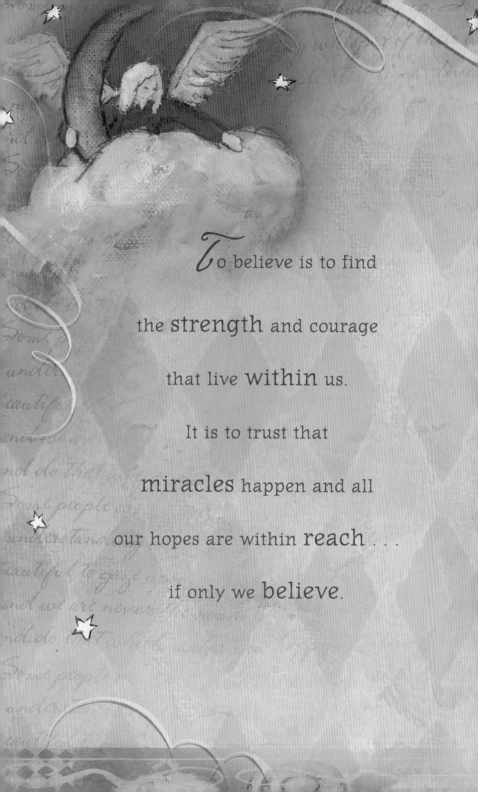

$\mathcal{T}$o believe is to find

the **strength** and courage

that live **within** us.

It is to trust that

miracles happen and all

our hopes are within **reach** . . .

if only we **believe**.

Hope and Healing

Be unafraid

to listen to your heart.

Within each of us

there is a spirit of hope

yearning to dance.

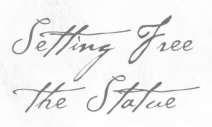

Setting Free the Statue

by Lisa Weedn

Life's changes had been too many, too sudden, too riddled with pain. I felt numb and frozen, trapped in my quiet despair. I could no longer hear the voice of my heart, instead I heard only a thundering silence. I wanted nothing more than to find the healing path and to regain my sense of self. I needed clarity and direction. I needed to find peace.

A friend of mine called and offered his sage advice. He recommended I take a *stomp*, which was his term for a therapeutic walk. He explained that whenever his shoulders weighed heavy, he set out for the woods, the city streets, the country paths. It mattered not where the physical journey took him, he claimed the act itself always cleared his mind, broke through his silence, and, most importantly, allowed him to "set free the statue." He's a man of metaphor, and the deeper meaning of his words always had the power to intrigue and challenge me. This friend of mine is very wise.

I lived in a small town of radiant beauty. My home and workplace were nestled between the mountains, the ocean, the art museum and the botanical gardens.

Each was less than a mile away, yet how long had it been since I tasted the ocean air, felt the crackle of leaves beneath my feet, or breathed in the inspiration of the masters. Far too long.

My practical mind told me I had no time for a walk, but my soul cried out, demanding attention. I'd only steal an hour, I promised myself. It would nourish me. Heeding the advice of my friend, I grabbed my sketchbook and pen and closed the door behind me. I didn't have a clue as to where I was going, but trusted I'd know when I arrived. And so it happened.

I decided to take the back streets, in hopes the charm of this city would lift my spirits. My pace was fast, too fast to truly appreciate the willow-lined paths that guarded my trail. My thoughts were too burdened to recognize what the moment was offering. My limbs felt heavy and stiff, my mind a chamber of tangled concerns, my heart still trapped in pain. I'm sure the briskness of my movements was a subconscious effort to set myself free. I was not yet aware of how significant this would be in the moments to come.

In less than fifteen minutes the sound of the wind in the trees was replaced by the rumble of a city street. I looked up to find myself facing the carved stone pillars of the art museum. A banner greeted me, claiming a Rodin exhibit. "Lovely," I sighed, amazed at how I had arrived here with so little memory of the journey. The sharp truth of this realization made me reach for my pen, and I scrawled out the words:

How often are we so preoccupied in our own private woes, our fears, our worries that we miss the beauty of the journey. Lift the veil. Pay attention. The landscape is so much larger than we can see.

Closing my book, I stepped into the lyrical hush of the museum walls. The scent of marble, bronze, and recently polished wooden floors teased my senses. Smiling guards stood at the corner of each room. Schoolchildren shuffled past quickly, whispering excitement over some exhibit in an adjacent hall. I deliberately began to pace my steps.

Room by room I stomped lightly. I felt as if I had entered a world of healing silence that I had almost forgotten to remember. What simple joy it was to hear the echo of my own footsteps. In some strange way, the sound was telling me that I was moving ahead, moving through, moving forward.

Ever so slowly, the peaceful voice inside of me was beginning to return, or perhaps I was just finally beginning to listen. But this, too, would not be rushed. Like a painting not yet finished, or a poem awaiting its final line, true insight has a way of delaying itself in times of shadow. I've come to believe this is part of the healing process. It takes a long while of ruminating on the painful angst of complexities before the soothing brilliance of simplicity surfaces.

My pace continued. I began to hear the faint rustling of passionate thought, contemplation wrapped in the voice of memory, a promising tune hinting at my future. Soon I found myself alone in a room with no doors, only open passageways leading into new rooms. How appropriate. I was taken by the symmetry of this concept, and once again I reached for my pen. Stumbling into a wooden bench, I sat, eyes to paper, my hand moving effortlessly across the page.

When heartache appears in our lives and we are forced to face bittersweet truths, we must be reminded that within each challenge there is always a higher offering. Although hidden from our view, we must raise our thinking, open our hearts, and recognize that we're being called to a new stage in life, a new room. Unfamiliarity can be frightening, and new paths are always a risk. But what is life, if not a journey into the wondrous unknown. Look around. Grace and beauty can be found even within pain. The only lock, keeping us trapped or blind or stuck, is fear. The only cage, our own minds.

When at last my pen had paused, I looked up to see the glory that surrounded me. I stood and began to drink in Rodin's studies, his sketches, his masterpieces, his legacy. I gazed at their beauty. I was moved by the myriad of feelings they evoked in me, trapped like in that of an ancient photograph, speaking to me in hushed undertones. Their effect was sublime, beckoning me to trace their exquisite form with my hands. Like a child, I was thrilled to have ignored the *Do Not Touch* warnings out of a passionate desire to feel. To experience. To know.

Then a thought came to me as my fingers met the coolness of the bronze and the marble. Although the feelings these sculptures summoned within me were warm, their touch was obviously that of stone. They spoke of life, yet they were lifeless. They conjured the illusion of movement, but they were immobile. Their vision made all in witness tremble in awe, but they could only claim a suspended reality. Certainly they deserved and received my praise and admiration. But a parallel could be drawn between their suspended reality and my being so stuck in my weighty world. This was a message I needed to hear.

Art is only feeling, and as Rodin himself said: *"The main point is to be moved, to love, to hope, to tremble, to live, but to be a man first."*

These were the final lines I wrote in my notebook before the clock on the wall told me it was time to leave. As I walked through the room, I spied yet another of Rodin's quotes laying open in a book I was clearly meant to see. *"In short, beauty is everywhere. It is not that it is lacking for our eyes to see, it is that our eyes fail to see it."* Indeed.

The walk back home was not a blind race with time. I strolled, I stomped, I took notice. My thoughts focused not on the pains and the darkness which I had let overpower me in recent days, instead I consciously made room for the light. The miracle of it all was that nothing had changed in my world, save for my own mindset, and this was proof enough that I had unlocked a door.

How easy it is to become trapped not only in heartache, but in the fear of moving forward. It took a simple stomp for me to learn that the gift of movement, even into uncharted territory, was one of life's greatest blessings. I had given myself permission to "set free the statue." I now understood the depth of my friend's metaphor, and the wondrous mystery of it all empowered me. I was inspired to take the risk of becoming more, for I was flesh, not stone. I was a dancer, not a statue. I was alive, and my passion for living had found its voice again.

Life

holds gifts

in its hands,

and gives them

to each of us

when it is time.

The Rose-Colored Chair

by Flavia Weedn

*W*e can be drawn to something as ordinary as an old chair because we need the gifts that it brings. Later, when it's time to give it up, we discover yet another gift.

The young man no longer needed the vintage 1930's chair. It had fulfilled its purpose, given him enjoyment, added a touch of style. He'd had the chair for years, and now it was time for him to move on, time to let it go.

He paid six dollars for it in a thrift shop fifteen years ago, this deep and thickly upholstered easy chair with the low cushioned back and wide curved arms. The fabric was a patterned velour, and through time most of its original wine color had faded to rose. The moment he first looked at it the young man knew it was classic.

When he moved from an apartment to a house, then back to an apartment, it moved with him. When his marriage dissolved, it remained steadfast and sturdy. This chair became his friend, his place to write, to read, and to sketch. Wherever he put it seemed to be the right place – at the end of a hall, the corner of his bedroom, or in the living room to the left of the fireplace. It always made a statement, reflecting a kind of significance in his life.

People were drawn to it. It was the kind of chair they remembered. Some thought it was the one in that Humphrey Bogart movie, the one where he was the detective. Others thought Cary Grant had sat on one of its arms in that old film with Katharine Hepburn.

To the young man's niece, it was a place of discovery. She would reach way down deep between the cushion and the sides and always find things. Usually small change, but sometimes treasures. She thought of it as her rose-colored chair.

For several months it was in the corner of the young man's office, bringing a certain unsuspected ambiance to the room. It was such an unusual piece that at first it caught his clients off-guard, but later most of them would slowly wander over to it, look closely at its lines, and eventually sit in the chair. If a chair could stand tall and proud, this one did. It embraced people and made them feel important.

His mother borrowed it for awhile. She had moved into a house with an office adjacent to her bedroom, and the chair was perfect. It fit beautifully in the corner beside the bookshelves, its faded rose color picked up the color of the flowers in the drapes. The look of it often brought back memories from another time, and when she sat in it, she felt warm and safe. It became her morning place where she could curl up, read the newspaper, drink her coffee, and begin her day. In the summer, it was her big white cat's favorite spot in the world. He loved to stretch out on one of the chair's arms and sleep there in the sun. Sometimes the cat rivaled her as to whose place it was.

The young man understood that it was more than a chair, more than a friend. That's what made it so special. Everyone needs a place to feel safe. A place that fits, feels right, a place where he or she belongs — or in a cat's case, a place in the sun.

When his mother moved, she didn't need the chair anymore and gave it back to him. He ran an ad in the newspaper, asked everyone he knew, and tried to sell or give it away to someone who would love it as much as he had. All who saw it thought it was an absolutely wonderful chair — it definitely had class, vintage and all that. However, no one seemed to need it enough to want to claim it as their own.

He called thrift shops, but no one wanted it. As a last resort, he knew he could always take it to the dump, but somehow he couldn't see himself going there. Not with the rose-colored chair. Finally, he had no choice, so reluctantly, he rented a pick-up truck and was now winding his way up the hill to the city dump, carrying it in the back. Seeing the chair in the rearview mirror, he was embarrassed that he felt the same twinge he felt the day he had to put his dog to sleep. How foolish, it's only a piece of furniture, he thought to himself and kept driving.

He followed the road, went through the gates, talked to the person in charge, and was directed to an area set aside for items other than trash. He was glad of that, because there was no way he could abandon this chair in a heap of garbage. As he was backing up the truck, he saw several people milling around, looking at other discarded furniture. One of the men walked over. He knew the man was interested; he could tell by the way he looked at the chair. The man was older, but otherwise reminded him of himself years ago when he'd first seen the chair in that thrift shop.

"It has great style. What a classic," the older man said, stroking the curve of the chair with his hands. "I have the perfect place for it. Do you think you could help me lift it into my truck?"

On his way home, the young man remembered how much he wanted to avoid taking the chair to the dump, but now his feelings had changed. He realized that it's not what the object is that matters, it's what it brings to you, what it does for you, and how it makes you feel. It was only a chair, but it had brought him enjoyment and style, and this made him feel good. To

his mother, it had brought beauty, memories, and a feeling of security. To his niece, it was a treasure hunt, filled with wonder. To his business clients, it had put their feet solidly on the ground and helped them relax. And now, to its new owner, the rose-colored chair would continue to give.

The young man had discovered a new truth, a new understanding. Life is all about time and the worth of the gifts it brings. It's about accepting when it's time to let go of something, so that it can continue to give to someone else in need of its gifts.

Now it was time for the rose-colored chair to move on, as it was for him. Life's circle was never-ending. This made him feel good inside.

Time

is a friend,

a healer,

a maker of

dreams.

Life's Mosaic

by Flavia Weedn

Time. It knows and tells all. It controls beginnings and endings, dreams and promises, truths and illusions. How incredible the wisdom held in its hands.

On the day she and her husband separated, the kitchen clock suddenly stopped running. A year later, on the day she filed for divorce, just as suddenly, it began running again. Who said there were no messages in small miracles.

She had wondered how it was that in such a short period of time a marriage which had lasted a lifetime of years could end. But that was dreams ago, and those months had walked away. Everything for her was new again. She was starting over. A little unsure, but proudly unafraid to take the next step.

She began to think of this time in her life as a kind of unfinished mosaic. Only when all the pieces were found and fit together would the image be visible. She was now in the process of moving on, aware that some of the pieces of her heart were still missing. But she was all right with that, she had found enough courage to begin again, and that had been the difficult part.

After the beginning was in place, the rest would slowly fit together. This much she knew.

She had closed one door and opened another, taking with her the things that mattered: memories, her capacity to love, her spirit, and her soul. Focusing on these, she was picking up pieces of her life, one by one. It would take time, but she knew the missing pieces would be found that same way, one by one.

Looking at time differently now, she would never take any of it for granted again. It had become a precious gift to her, she savored its full measure, tried to make it all count. With its help, she was seeing more of the essence of who she was and that which defined her. Time was now a part of her life.

She felt proud of the choices, decisions and judgments she was making. The teacher side of her was gentle, knowing all the while that decisions are not irrevocable and choices can be changed. Not rushing, she taught herself slowly, carefully, aware of her fragile vulnerability.

The student in her soaked up the knowledge, for she was eager to learn, anxious to discover. She would never reach back, or try to re-live yesterday, instead she'd remember the gifts it had brought and hold on to them until all traces of emptiness were gone. She was learning the importance of forgiving herself and accepting the truth that whatever someone else did was not her fault. The closing of this chapter of her life had begun.

To finally let go of the weight of the hurt she had felt made her feel free and lifted her spirit. By allowing her heart spontaneity, she found that singing loudly off-key in her car and dancing barefoot in the moonlight with her granddaughter gifted her soul. She listened to music more and kept vases filled with fresh flowers — knowing all the while that they were there for her alone to see. Appropriate enough. However, she was not entirely alone — she had found someone. She had found herself.

Renting a smaller house in a different area of town brought her the warmth and geniality of a quiet old neighborhood. It put her in touch again with some of the simple things she'd almost forgotten — picking fruit from the trees, a neighbor greeting her in the mornings, another handing her roses through a fence.

She awakened to the freshness of the ocean air, the whisper of its breeze, and the faint early sounds of church bells. Children's laughter lightened her afternoons, and in the early evenings she watched backyard birds drink from the birdbath under the pomegranate tree. She found small joys in the experiences of these ordinary days, and drawing upon this, felt of value again. She was beginning to heal.

Thankful for all the blessings God had given her, those she treasured most were her children and grandchild. She cherished them dearly, loved them completely and let them know it no matter what their age. Her reason for living, they propelled her into the tomorrows of her days, and she felt more alive each day because of them. They were gifts to her.

In addition to her children, she was grateful for being involved with a work she loved. This was a different kind of love, but one she also met with a passion. It was important to her, not just for her ability to make a living, but because it enabled her to stay close to her feelings, her philosophy, and the heart she still wore on her sleeve. It made her feel real.

Her work represented that which she was a part of — that which she knew intimately, spiritually. Through this, she recognized that her passion for life was responsible for the development of the artist within her. It brought her joy, and her soul needed to feel joy. No matter how swiftly life moved, she would not let herself forget this. Another piece of the image had been found.

Although not particularly analytical, she had discovered her own simple strengths, and realized that she didn't have to be everything, just herself. No longer trying to live moment to moment, she had become conscious of her existence. She had found new meaning in her life, and knew that no matter how hard life is, it is of great value and worth living.

She believed in hope, love, and the courage of her spirit, and knew that whatever was to happen in her future would not happen by chance. She had faith in something larger and more wondrous than life. God, she thought, was taking time to guide her, especially through this September part of her journey.

Making a commitment to herself, she had promised her heart not to miss any of the small joys as she lived these days of her life. She vowed to continue to appreciate the real beauty found in the wonder and experience of living.

Singing to music on the radio, she put a single garden gladiola in a vase and brought out her bright pottery dishes. She was unveiling more of her life every day. With her heart, she could almost see the mosaic beginning to form — its image would include all the pieces of her heart and soul, and show her spirit dancing as free and as beautiful as she imagined. It would be worthy of all she'd dreamed.

She knew that somewhere in time the pieces would all fit together. She also knew that this time in her life was meant for her. With the ticking of the clock on the wall, she placed a setting for one at the kitchen table and sat down to dinner.

Hope is the

silent strength

within the heart

that never stops

believing.

A Hand to Hold

by Lisa Weedn

Sylvie was eighteen months old when she picked up her first paintbrush. Dipping it into a jar of thick wet color, she stared at the easel in front of her, then down at the newsprint she stood upon. Without hesitation, she ignored the easel and began large fluid strokes on the paper surrounding her feet. I looked on in awe. She was tasting the first sweet drops of creative freedom.

Sylvie giggled with each brush stroke, enthralled in a world all her own. Finally, her face and body covered in paint, she stood back, smiled up at me, and with pride said "Look!" She was heaven to witness. I passionately applauded and quickly retrieved her masterpiece from the floor. This was a moment to be savored forever.

That night, after her painting had dried, I trimmed off the edges and began to position it in a frame. I turned it to the right, to the left, then sideways. That's when I saw the miracle. My little one had painted an angel. A wondrous vision, striking and very clear. In my excitement, I summoned my daughter into the room. I asked, "Baby, did you know you painted an angel?"

She nodded and replied, "My angel. Pretty angel. She holds my hand." I whisked Sylvie up in my arms and said a prayer of thanks that God had granted me the privilege of being her mother.

Sylvie started talking when she was less than a year old. She was articulate beyond her years and had a spiritual air about her, so her comment didn't surprise me. But it did capture my attention. I loved the notion of an angel holding her hand. I loved that she found peace in the thought. I loved even more that we both believed it to be true.

A year passed and Sylvie grew from being a toddler to a pre-schooler of animated enthusiasm and delight. She was known for her impromptu remarks of wisdom, and for her ability to embrace life with curiosity, clarity and love.

Alas, just before the holidays, we began to notice her radiant smile fade into lapses of blank stares. At first, we misunderstood them to be daydreaming. We even thought them dear, charming, and the product of her creative soul — until they increased in frequency and her little body began to tremble into states of unconsciousness. It was then we introduced her to the medical team of sterile white coats, needle probes, and the *monster machines,* as she called them. To watch an innocent endure pain and fear is nothing short of agony. It was a dark and most terrifying time in our lives.

The worst was ruled out, thank God, and albeit painful, on some level we were relieved to finally learn of her diagnosis. We were told she was experiencing *absence seizures*, over one hundred per day. Each would last just short of two minutes, but they were the longest two minutes we had ever known. I remember sitting in the neurologist's office, my heart breaking, my mind calculating how much time my precious girl was losing. The reality left me numb. Sadness and disbelief consumed me.

It was hard to tell what was going on inside her. So young was she, so fragile she had suddenly become. Sylvie had no memory of the seizures, only the knowledge that one moment she'd be with us, and the next she'd be in an unknown void — only to return as quickly as she had left. She was confused. So were we.

What followed was a path new to all of us. Our goal was to gain as much control over the seizures as we possibly could and to make her childhood the joyful journey it was meant to be. We were told she had a fifty percent chance of growing out of this condition within ten years. This gave us hope, and we chose to believe only the best. We held tightly to the hand of faith.

Then came the daily medications, the side effects, the marked change in this bright spirit's young life. We fully recognized that the nightmare could have been so much worse, but the fact remained that this was still a nightmare. We took our days and our dreams one moment at a time, filling the lucid periods with as much happiness, and as little fear, as possible.

Sylvie proved to be more than courageous. Over the next few years she became a master at hiding her tears behind that radiant smile. Bravely, she accepted the thick pink medicinal liquid that made her stomach knot and her mind race at such high speed that sleep was a luxury. She learned to never ride a bike, take a bath, or swim without someone watching her constantly. She found ways to make jokes with her friends about her daily emergency trips to the bathroom, where they'd find her violently throwing up. Many times she didn't make it to the bathroom. It took a strong, faithful spirit to take it all in stride. Sylvie was, and is, no less.

Throughout this time, I did what every parent would do. I showered Sylvie with all the love in my heart. I encouraged her to talk freely, openly. I gave her what answers I could whenever she asked, and I allowed her room for blessed silence. In my private hours I researched and educated myself. I educated her teachers, caregivers, and the parents of her friends. I spoke with others whose children shared Sylvie's condition. None of them offered much reassurance. Most had resigned themselves, saying: "There'll be some good days and some very bad days. You learn to

live with it." But for me, resignation was not the answer. Hope was.

I would hold Sylvie's hair back and stroke her forehead as her body lurched. I would whisper to her that she was safe and that everything was going to be all right. I would promise her that we would find a way, together. I would hold her in the midst of a seizure and ask for God's guidance. Where did she go during these times? Was it a dark, empty place? I prayed it was a place of gentle peace and bright light. I had to believe it was.

Sylvie is six now. We've been told that she needs to undergo a battery of new tests. The doctors warn us that she may have a condition which offers less than the originally promised odds. We can only hold on to faith.

This morning we ready ourselves for a trip to see a new team of neurologists. The day promises sterile white coats, far too many needle probes, and monster machines, as she still calls them. Each of us is nervous, though we try to hide it behind pillow fights and pancakes. The hour approaches, and Sylvie gallantly slips on her favorite bell bottoms and Spice Girls tee shirt. I smile and tell her how beautiful she is. I fix her hair, and we share a moment of silence, each of us deep in thought.

She breaks the silence with "Mama, don't be

afraid. I'm not. Did I tell you what I want to be when I grow up? So many things. I want to be a fairy, a pediatrician, a lilac, a big, beautiful tree." My tears begin to fall. I hide them as I whisk her lanky body into my arms and once again say a prayer of thanks that God has granted me the privilege of being her mother.

We begin to walk out the door. She stops and runs back into her room, returning with a small framed painting that sits next to her bed — a magical image painted by an eighteen-month-old bright spirit. I smile at her and say, "Ah, your angel. Good, baby, both she and I will hold your hand today."

"Mama," she says softly, "my angel never lets go of my hand. I brought her for you."

I feel a blanket of hope embrace me. Love, and her exquisite constancy, is the very source of our strength. And the hand each of us holds — the one offered through every challenge and heartache, along every path life takes us — is the hand of faith.

Forever, let us hold on tight.

To the Reader

Heartache is a part of the living experience. It touches us all and can be felt on many levels — from a tragic loss to a private personal passage. Each time we feel the ache, we are being challenged to grow, to learn, and to better love ourselves and others. Faith, forgiveness, acceptance, and the courage to go on embracing life's gift, are all a part of the path we are being called to take. At times we must move slowly and deliberately through the process, other times we have no choice but to step into the new without warning or preparation. But the human spirit is miraculous in its capacity to heal, for it is made of hope and strength and an undeniable power of love.

In writing this book, we walked down the path of memory. We cried the tears and tasted life twice. There were many experiences that didn't make it into this book, simply because there were not enough pages to tell all. Yet the stories that did find their way here were chosen because they touched upon the clearest light of hope we could offer. In every case, the heartache we experienced caused a new window of understanding to open in our lives and in our hearts — helping us to become more, never less.

We hope that you have found a story or two that has allowed you to feel that you are never walking the path alone. We hope that you have heard echoes of comfort within the sadness, and most of all, we hope that you will forever hold on to the hand of faith, for it is offered to one and all, within every moment of light or shadow.

Gentle blessings,

Flavia and Lisa Weedn

Flavia

Lisa and her daughter Sylvie

Photos by Chris Chandler

Flavia Weedn is one of America's leading contemporary inspirational writers and illustrators. Offering hope for the human spirit, Flavia portrays the basic excitement, simplicity and beauty she sees in the ordinary things of life. Her work has touched the lives of millions for over three decades.

Lisa Weedn, Flavia's daughter and co-author, shares her mother's philosophy and passion. For over fifteen years, Lisa's writings have been a quiet messenger of the fundamental truth that age has no barrier on feelings of the human heart.

Their collaborative work, which celebrates life and embraces meaningful core values, can be found in numerous books, collections of fine stationery goods, giftware, and lifestyle products distributed worldwide.

Flavia and Lisa live in Santa Barbara, California.